WHAT'S INSIDE

#1 Have an 'Attitude of Gratitude'

#2 Gratitude is good for you!

#3 Gratitude turns what you have into enough

#4 Life is your adventure!

#5 "I am lucky"

#6 "Thank you"

#7 Be grateful for life's 'silver linings'

#8 "I am grateful for my body"

#9 The universe gives you gifts

#10 Start and end the day with a grateful heart

WHAT IS GRATITUDE?

Gratitude is the world's most powerful tool for creating happiness and making life beautiful.

It's realising there is always something or someone to be thankful for, and being happy with what you have without needing more.

It's choosing to look at everything with a positive attitude.

LIFE IS MUCH BETTER WHEN YOU PRACTICE...
GRATITUDE.

#2

Gratitude is good for you!

Practicing gratitude is really good for you.
Try it out yourself to see the magic it can do.

The more you practice it, the more you'll find...
it has the power to give you a happy body and mind.

THINK OF GRATITUDE LIKE A POWERFUL DAILY VITAMIN.

Focus on the things you have, not what you think you need.
Gratitude makes what you have enough, with happiness guaranteed.

Notice all the good in your life, whether BIG or small.
You can be happy with what you have right now by feeling thankful for it ALL.

Challenge

PICK A ROOM IN YOUR HOUSE TO SIT IN.

TAKE TIME TO NOTICE WHAT'S AROUND YOU TO BE THANKFUL FOR.

Write it down

Other ways to notice...

KEEP A GRATITUDE JOURNAL OR NOTEBOOK AND TRY TO WRITE IN IT DAILY.

WRITE DOWN WHAT YOU ARE THANKFUL FOR; THIS COULD BE A PERSON? A PLACE? A GAME?

Draw it out

TRY DRAWING THE THINGS YOU ARE THANKFUL FOR! DISPLAY THEM ON THE WALL TO REMIND YOU.

Don't focus on what other people have or what they get to do, choose to look at all the good in YOUR life and be grateful you get to be YOU!

You always have everything you need to be happy, it's a choice you can make in your mind.
Be thankful for whatever comes your way and leave jealously behind.

"LIFE IS YOUR ADVENTURE, IT IS NOT A COMPETITION."

IMPORTANT!

IT'S *okay* TO FEEL JEALOUS, IT IS A VERY NORMAL FEELING.
BUT, IT IS POSSIBLE TO WORK THROUGH IT USING GRATITUDE.

IF YOU START TO COMPARE YOURSELF TO OTHERS, **STOP** & FOCUS ON THE GOOD THINGS YOU ALREADY HAVE.

Nobody is you and that is your power!

You are powerful and unique just as you are!

- HOW WOULD YOU DESCRIBE YOURSELF IN 3 WORDS?

- WHAT DO YOU LOVE ABOUT BEING YOU?

- ASK SOMEONE WHAT THEY THINK MAKES YOU SPECIAL.

Try this: Pick one of these affirmations and repeat it 3 times.
'I am unique'
'I am my biggest fan'
'I am loved'

It's easy to take for granted the things you have access to in your day.
Like food, clean water and a safe place to live and play.

Noticing how lucky you are
and all that you have to be thankful for,
will make you feel blessed and want to help those less fortunate much

MORE.

Things you are lucky to have...

 **Electricity to keep all of your electronic devices working.**

CAN YOU NAME SOME ITEMS THAT USE ELECTRICITY IN YOUR HOME?

 **A place to live.**

Clean water to drink and wash with.

People who love and care for you.

 **Toys to play with and books to read.**

 **Healthy food to eat.**

How can you help people less fortunate?

DONATE GIFTS, OR TOYS YOU DON'T PLAY WITH ANYMORE TO A CHARITY SHOP OR A CHILDREN'S HOSPITAL.

HAVE A ONE IN, ONE OUT RULE WHEN GETTING SOMETHING NEW,

E.G. DONATE A TOY, BOOK OR AN ITEM OF CLOTHING EVERY TIME YOU GET A NEW ONE.

AS A FAMILY LOOK INTO HOW TO SPONSOR A CHILD IN NEED.

ORGANISE A FAMILY FUNDRAISER AND PICK A CHARITY TO DONATE THE FUNDS TO.

<u>THINGS YOU CAN GIVE FOR FREE</u>
A SMILE, YOUR FRIENDSHIP, HUGS, YOUR KINDNESS & LOVE.
CAN YOU THINK OF ANY MORE?

#6

"Thank you."

"Merci" (FRENCH)

"Gracias" (SPANISH)

"Mahalo" (HAWAIIAN)

"Spasiba" (RUSSIAN)

HOW TO SAY 'THANK YOU' IN SOME OTHER LANGUAGES.

YOU CAN ALSO SAY THANK YOU USING ACTIONS SUCH AS; A HUG, A THUMBS UP, A FRIENDLY NOD, A HIGH 5, A LETTER OR A DRAWING.

Saying thank you shows you're grateful for what someone has done for you.
You don't always have to use your words, you can show it with actions too.

Always look out for acts of kindness whether BIG or small.
Saying thanks makes people happy, it's a word that's magical.

Tip:
EVEN IF YOU DON'T LIKE SOMETHING THAT YOU'VE BEEN GIFTED, IT'S GOOD TO SAY THANK YOU, FOR THE TIME, EFFORT, AND THOUGHT THAT WENT INTO IT.

Some ways you can say thank you...

 SEND A THANK YOU CARD OR LETTER.

GIVE A HUG.

MAKE A YUMMY TREAT TO GIFT SOMEONE.

GET CREATIVE, DRAW A PICTURE OR MAKE SOMETHING.

SHARE YOUR TOYS OR LEND A BOOK.

'Thank you Friday'

EACH FRIDAY WRITE A THANK YOU NOTE FOR SOMEONE WHO HAS HELPED YOU OR SOMEONE YOU'RE THANKFUL FOR.

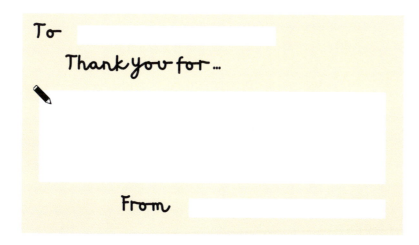

& Remember to...

SAY THANK YOU TO THE PEOPLE IN YOUR COMMUNITY WHO HELP YOU.

E.G. TEACHERS, BUS DRIVERS, DOCTORS, DENTISTS, POSTAL WORKERS, SHOP ASSISTANTS.

#1

> Be grateful for life's silver linings.

A 'SILVER LINING' IS SOMETHING THAT GIVES YOU COMFORT OR HOPE IN AN UNHAPPY SITUATION.

(ASK A GROWN UP TO SHARE SOME EXAMPLES).

Look for reasons to smile through
whatever life may bring.
Gratitude will help you find the positive
in everything.

Mistakes and hard times can help you grow
and make you who you
are today.

So try to find a silver lining when
challenges come
your way.

'FIND SOMETHING POSITIVE' SOME EXAMPLES...

RAIN MEANS I CAN WEAR WELLIES AND JUMP IN PUDDLES.

MAKING A MISTAKE TEACHES ME SOMETHING NEW.

BEING POORLY ISN'T FUN. BUT, IT SHOWS ME HOW MUCH MY FAMILY & FRIENDS CARE.

The 'Reframe Game.'

Use the 'Yes' → 'But' method.

e.g.

YES, THE PITCH IS FLOODED SO I CAN'T GO TO FOOTBALL PRACTICE.
BUT, I AM THANKFUL I CAN PRACTICE AT HOME INSTEAD.

YES, I DON'T HAVE ENOUGH MONEY FOR THE TOY I WANT.
BUT, I AM VERY LUCKY TO GET POCKET MONEY AND CAN KEEP SAVING OR PICK SOMETHING ELSE.

YES, I MISS MY PET GERBIL.
BUT, I AM GRATEFUL FOR THE MOMENTS WE SHARED TOGETHER.

YOU CAN DO IT!

GIVE IT A GO!

#8

> I am grateful for my body.

Your body is so incredible and something to be grateful for.
It's a huge gift to be alive with the whole world to explore.

Your body has five powerful senses: sight, hearing, smell, taste and touch.

So, give thanks and be kind to your body because it helps you
do so much!

ACTIVITY

NOT EVERYONE IS ABLE TO USE ALL OF THEIR 5 SENSES. EXPLORE WHAT TOOLS AND METHODS SENSORY IMPAIRED CHILDREN USE TO SUPPORT THEIR LEARNING.

Each healthy organ and limb is a gift!

Show it thanks and love by keeping your body healthy and strong.

EAT A BALANCED DIET, INCLUDE LOTS OF FRUIT AND VEGETABLES!

BE ACTIVE!

DRINK PLENTY OF WATER.

▸ SCIENTISTS ESTIMATE THAT THE HUMAN NOSE CAN RECOGNISE A TRILLION DIFFERENT SCENTS!

▸ YOUR BRAIN KEEPS WORKING EVEN WHEN YOU'RE ASLEEP. IT SENDS THE SIGNALS THAT MAKE YOUR HEART BEAT AND YOUR LUNGS DRAW IN BREATH.

▸ A HUMAN HEART BEATS AROUND 100,000 TIMES PER DAY.

A NIGHT TIME MEDITATION TO SAY THANK YOU TO YOUR BODY.

ASK A PARENT OR LOVED ONE TO READ THIS TO YOU BEFORE YOU GO TO SLEEP.

Make sure you are comfy and somewhere quiet, ready to listen and relax.

ALL BODIES ARE SPECIAL, UNIQUE AND BEAUTIFUL AND YOURS HAS WORKED HARD ALL DAY LONG.

LET US THANK SOME AMAZING BODY PARTS ONE BY ONE, STARTING WITH YOUR TOES. THANK YOUR TOES FOR HELPING YOU STAND UP TALL AND FOR KEEPING YOU BALANCED TODAY. GIVE THEM A WIGGLE AND SAY 'THANK YOU TOES'.

NEXT, LET'S THANK YOUR STRONG LEGS THAT HAVE BEEN BUSY TODAY, RUNNING JUMPING AND DANCING.
GIVE THEM BOTH A LITTLE SHAKE AND SAY 'THANK YOU LEGS'.

PLACE YOUR HANDS ON YOUR TUMMY, THANK YOUR TUMMY FOR HOLDING ALL THE YUMMY FOOD YOU'VE EATEN TODAY AND FOR TURNING IT INTO ENERGY TO LEARN AND PLAY.
RUB YOUR TUMMY GENTLY AND SAY 'THANKYOU. TUMMY'.

FIND YOUR HEART NOW, HOLD ONE HAND ON YOUR HEART AND FEEL ITS STRONG BEAT. THANK YOUR HEART FOR BEING OPEN TO GRATITUDE TODAY AND SAY 'THANK YOU HEART'.

NEXT, JUMP A FINGER UP TO YOUR NOSE.
THANK YOUR NOSE FOR HELPING YOU TO BREATHE AND FOR ALLOWING YOU TO SMELL, GIVE IT A WIGGLE AND SAY 'THANK YOU NOSE'.

LASTLY, LET'S THANK YOUR EYES, THANK YOUR EYES FOR LOOKING OUT FOR YOU TODAY.
THANK THEM FOR LETTING YOU SEE YOUR FRIENDS, FAMILY, TOYS, DRAWINGS AND THE WORLD AROUND YOU.
CLOSE THEM NOW, LET THEM REST AND SAY 'THANK YOU EYES'.

GIVE YOUR BODY ONE FINAL BIG THANK YOU BY GIVING YOURSELF A NICE TIGHT HUG. REST YOUR BODY NOW SO IT'S READY FOR A DAY FULL OF ADVENTURE TOMORROW.

When you slow down it's easier to notice the universe is continually giving.
Happiness can always be found from the beautiful world
you live in.

You'll always find something to be grateful for with the outside world as your playground.
A muddy puddle, a climbable tree,
or a streams nice calming sound.

Q. WHAT HAS THE UNIVERSE GIFTED YOU TODAY?

TAKE A 'GRATITUDE WALK'

TAKE A WALK WITH YOUR FAMILY. TRY TO WALK AS QUIETLY AS POSSIBLE SO YOU CAN NOTICE EVERYTHING AROUND YOU USING ALL YOUR SENSES.

DO YOU ENJOY THE SOUND OF BIRDS?
SEE A SPIDERS WEB?
IS THE AIR COOLING YOU DOWN?
WHAT CAN YOU SMELL?

GIVE THANKS FOR ALL YOU NOTICED.

GIFTS FROM NATURE

 THE SUN THAT WARMS YOU.

 THE FOOD THAT THE EARTH PROVIDES.

 THE WATER YOU DRINK.

CAN YOU NAME ANY MORE?

A PRAYER TO THE EARTH

'THANK YOU EARTH, I AM SO GRATEFUL TO YOU FOR GIVING ME FRESH AIR TO BREATHE, BEAUTIFUL SIGHTS TO SEE AND FOR SUPPORTING MY FEET.'

WRITE YOUR OWN IF YOU LIKE.

WALK OR RIDE A BIKE WHERE POSSIBLE INSTEAD OF GOING IN A CAR, IT IS BETTER FOR YOU AND THE EARTH.

TURN OFF THE TV AND ANY LIGHTS WHEN YOU LEAVE A ROOM.

LEARN WHICH HOUSEHOLD ITEMS YOU CAN RECYCLE.

How can you show thanks to the earth?

PLANT A TREE.

TURN OFF THE TAP WHEN YOU ARE BRUSHING YOUR TEETH.

USE BOTH SIDES OF A SHEET OF PAPER.

GRAB A BIN BAG AND GLOVES AND GO ON A FAMILY OUTING TO COLLECT ANY LITTER YOU SEE.

Now you know all about gratitude, make practicing it a daily thing.

Pick a time every day to be grateful, you'll be surprised by the happiness it can bring.

IDEAS ON HOW TO FIT GRATITUDE INTO YOUR DAY.

- Use a daily gratitude journal.
- Take turns to name something you are grateful for at the same time daily. This could be at dinnertime, on your journey to or from school, or at bedtime.
- Be thankful for a new day each morning when you wake.
- Make a gratitude jar. (Write something you are grateful for on a piece of paper whenever you like and put it in the jar, at the end of the year open them all!)

21 DAY GRATITUDE CHALLENGE

CHALLENGE: NAME SOMETHING YOU ARE GRATEFUL FOR <u>EVERY DAY</u> FOR 21 DAYS. COLOUR IN AS YOU GO.

*SOME SCIENTISTS HAVE SAID IT TAKES 21 DAYS TO FORM A HABIT!

GOOD EFFORT, YOU'RE DOING GREAT.

LET'S MAKE IT A HABIT, KEEP GOING.

YOU DID IT, BE PROUD. YOU HAVE THE POWER TO BE GRATEFUL!

HOORAY

This book is presented solely for advice and entertainment purposes.
The information provided is designed to provide helpful information on the subject discussed.

The content is the sole expression and opinion of its authors, You are responsible for your own choices, actions, and results.

All contents copyright © 2020 Toni McAree and protected under the UK copyright, designs and patents act 1988.
All rights reserved worldwide.

Printed in Great Britain
by Amazon